# MASTER YOUR EMOTIONS:

The simple guide to master your stress,

negativity and worries,

thus transforming your life.

Oliver Bennet

# Table of Contents

Please consult a licensed professional before attempting any techniques outlined in this book.

By reading this document, the reader agrees that under no circumstances is the author responsible for any losses, direct or indirect, which are incurred as a result of the use of information contained within this document, including, but not limited to, — errors, omissions, or inaccuracies.

# Chapter 1:    Assessing Your Emotions

Assessing your emotional state is a key step in honing emotional intelligence and having empathy in general. Some people may be constantly cued into their emotional states, while some others may go a day or a week without thinking about it at all.

## Why Do Emotions Often Take Control Of People?

### People Don't Recognize Own Emotions As A Staging Ground

Recognizing your own emotions is the staging ground for recognizing the emotions of others. This is why empathy and emotional intelligence do not consist of single emotional skills, but several. This should lead people to understand that successful emotional intelligence involves tying several emotional steps together to interconnectivity. If all you are doing is recognizing your own emotions, you do not understand others' emotions, and you are ultimately not behaving with emotional intelligence.

### People Don't Know How To Control Feelings

Our feelings are expressions of our emotional and mental state of existence. Normally tied to our physical and social sensory feeling, they are used to react to joy, fear, love, disgust, sadness, hate, pleasure, and a host of other emotions. In other to prevent extreme behaviors which usually comes at high costs, we must control and suppress some emotions and feelings.

Persons who cannot generally control their feelings engage in unwarranted acts of violence, fighting, unprotected sex, and abuse of different substances which will undoubtedly put their lives at risks. There is a wide range of factors that contribute to such lack of control apart from the mind's feelings. These factors include environmental, genetically, social, and biological factors.

## People Don't Understand The Impact Of Emotions

There is an active connection between how you feel and the physical problems you experience, and this is because you are not different from how you feel. Most of the challenges you experienced in the past or those you are facing now have solid connections with your dominant emotional pattern.

When emotions are used in the right way, they can become a tool for empowerment, and when they are misused or repressed, they can become a gateway to suffering. Many people are afraid to maintain a positive emotion for a long time. They have accepted the mistaken idea that life cannot be so exciting enough for anyone to be happy all the time.

You need to start dealing with your emotions so that you can identify and get rid of the negative ones while embracing the positive ones. All these discussions we are having about feelings and problems are so important.

### Signs of Emotionally Unstable People

Feelings, especially intense feelings, can often be autonomous, which means they are automatic and subconscious, developing due to an external force or trigger.

To take control of our emotional selves, we must learn the signs of emotionally unstable people.

### Denial

Denial is the rejection to accept the truth of a situation, and in short-term use, it is a healthy and effective coping mechanism. It

2

allows the unconscious mind to deal with the situation before the conscious mind must deal with it. However, persistent denial can cause severe emotional distress; we all know that ignoring a problem will not solve it. Denial prevents us from dealing with our emotions and seeking support because we cannot face the issue. It is so powerful; you may not even realize you are in denial until someone else helps you see it.

## Being Overly Serious

Being too serious detaches you from your coworkers and friends. Nobody wants to say something funny they found online to you, because they would come off as not serious. You unknowingly miss out on the beautiful things in life, and it might begin to reflect on your family and kids.

## Going through Your Phone in the Middle of a Conversation

This is a very disrespectful act that is unfortunately very common nowadays. Some people are so attached to their phone that they can't bear to take their eyes off it for an hour; hence they tend to go through their phone even when an important meeting is going on. This can mess up your relationship because it makes the person think you're insensitive. Bringing out your phone and going through it in the middle of a conversation is not only insensitive, but it's disrespectful too. You're telling the person that whatever they were saying to you, as important as it was to them, is unimportant to you, and that can make the person feel insignificant. You should discontinue using your phone in the middle of a conversation.

## Calling The Names Of The Important People You Know

If you cannot go through a conversation without mentioning the names of the important people you know, this is you trying to make yourself look better than every other person sitting in that room at that moment, and you do not necessarily have to drag that kind of attention to yourself. You have met the president—nice. Your father's brother is the one on TV—yeah, that's nice. Not everyone needs to know. Instead of making you look interesting, you come off as a braggart in want of attention and that sincerely puts people off. Name dropping might make you feel better about yourself, but how do you think it will make others feel about you?

## Subtle Bragging

Subtle bragging, or humble bragging, is the act of bragging in a way that is not exactly noticed as bragging. You don't realize you are bragging when you practice humble bragging, because by your standards you are just modest. This is something we do among friends, sometimes innocently.

## Screaming At People

No one likes a screamer. No matter how much the person deserves your screaming, it's not necessary. You make people feel small and insignificant when you scream at them, especially when it is a constant habit to scream when you are mad at others.

## Gossiping

When you gossip about another person, it says more about you than it does about the person you talked about. It doesn't make sense to base your discussion on another's life; relationships that thrive on gossip have a very shaky foundation and are bound to crash sooner than later. Gossiping is a horrible habit, and it depicts a very low state of emotional intelligence.

## Talking A Lot More Than Listening

When you talk more than you listen, it limits your chances at learning and unlearning things. You are shoving your opinion down others' throat without giving them the time or the chance to air theirs.

Listening most times helps you to make a better decision. Not listening to people when they talk and being too concerned about airing your own opinion will make you look ignorant. At some point, you will begin to say things that do not make a lot of sense because you were not listening in the first place. You will suddenly begin to look ignorant, and no one wants to associate with an ignorant person who is also unwilling to learn.

## Posting Too Much Of Yourself On Social Media

A lot of people are guilty of this action. It depicts a want for acceptance, and it's usually captured by the phrase "putting it all out there." Well, news flash, you do not have to do this. You do not necessarily have to tell the world all the dreams you have or everything you do after you wake up and before you go to bed. You do not have to be validated by social media and those online. They don't care that much about you. They should not know so much about you. It's needless throwing these things in their faces. Save some information for yourself. Remember, the internet has a good memory; it never forgets.

## Saying Too Much Of Yourself Too Early In A Relationship

Not everyone needs to know all the information you spill to them when you talk to them for the first time. Sharing too much too early makes you come off as an attention seeker. It seems like you want the person to think you are real and open and want them to like you almost immediately. It's a lot better to let the relationship flow organically, and then the rest of the information will come out naturally without stress. It's also better to relax and know the other person better while building trust in the relationship. Sharing too much of yourself is rushing things and does not give the other person a chance to be comfortable.

**Being Closed-Minded**

This is a huge problem. You must view things with an open mind. Keeping a closed mind makes you unapproachable. It also means that you already have a formed opinion about a certain thing. When you are approached, you are unwilling to listen and make changes to your initial thoughts, making you inaccessible. It's very practical to keep an open mind and be open to changes. These habits are associated with people with low emotional intelligence, and they should be stopped now. They are harmful to you, the people around you, and your emotional intelligence growth.

**Avoidance**

Avoidance is similar to denial, but it is much more conscious. It happens when we cope with certain events, emotions, or thoughts by avoiding them altogether. For example, a person experiencing high levels of work stress may stop showing up for work. We avoid stressors in hopes of eliminating that stress, but this causes more stress and more discomfort because we are not dealing with the emotional trigger.

## Social Withdrawal

Many people experiencing emotional turmoil will withdraw from family and friends. This is not to be mixed up with simply needing some alone time, which we all need sometimes. Social withdrawal happens when we feel too exhausted, overwhelmed, or insecure about being around people whose company we once enjoyed. Human beings crave connection, but it is easy to fall into withdrawal, increasing negative emotions like loneliness and self-doubt.

## Compulsive Behavior

Compulsive behavior is the repeated engagement in an activity despite sense and reason, usually to the point of obsession. We engage in this behavior because it can provide temporary relief against negative emotions like anxiety, stress, and grief. Still, it can exacerbate these problems by leaving us feeling out of control of our behaviors. Examples of compulsive behavior include binge-eating, over-exercising, hoarding, gambling, and sex. For those struggling with Obsessive-Compulsive Disorder, these activities may seem very simple and insignificant, like hand-washing, checking (doors, gas taps, light switches, etc.), ordering/organizing, and counting.

## Self-Destructive Behavior

Sometimes, we find relief from negative emotions through behaviors that are temporarily pleasurable but ultimately self-destructive. A great example of self-destructive behavior is smoking cigarettes despite knowing it can cause health problems later in life. We are often conscious of this kind of behavior's negative consequences, but we engage in it anyway for the relief it provides. Common self-destructive behaviors include smoking, alcohol abuse, drug abuse, binge-eating, and self-harm.

# Chapter 2:    How To Use Your Emotions To Grow

Emotion is a psychological state generated subconsciously. Certain internal or external bodily responses stimulate it. Sometimes, people interchangeably use the words' emotions and moods together, but there are differences in meaning. An emotion is intense, short-lived, and has a cause. On the other hand, a mood may not have a definite cause, is milder, and could last longer.

## Basic Emotions And How To Use Them To Grow And Change Our Lives

Emotions come in different types and influence what we do and interact. Most decisions we take are based on our present emotions. Psychologist Paul Eckman in the 1970s identified six universally basic emotions: anger, surprise, fear, disgust, sadness, and happiness. Later on, he added excitement, embarrassment, shame, and pride.

He later came up with another theory that worked like a color wheel blending some of these basic emotions to create others, such as trust and joy to create love.

Below, we identify some of these basic emotions and their effect on our daily lives and behavior.

## Happiness

Most people strive to achieve this emotion called happiness. It is an emotional state of feeling pleasant brought about by feelings of well-being, satisfaction, gratification, joy, and contentment. It is expressed through:

·    A smiling face

- Having a relaxed stance

- Pleasant tone on your voice

Happiness is considered as a basic human emotion. Things that influence happiness in people are normally culture. For example, attaining some high standards in life like owning property and having a good job could result in happiness. However, the truth is that happiness is dependent on personal belief, and what may bring happiness to one may not necessarily mean anything to another.

Happiness and health are related. Ill health can deprive one of the emotions of happiness. Both mental and physical health contributes to emotions of happiness. Also, to be noted, marital satisfaction is a great contributor to emotions of happiness.

Emotions of happiness are linked to poor health, anxiety, stress, loneliness, and depression. This has brought about lowered immunity, inflammations, and a decrease in life expectancy to such individuals.

**Sadness**

Sadness is a transient emotion characterized by bad feelings of disinterest, hopelessness, grief, disappointment, and dampened mood. Emotions of sadness happen to everyone from time to time. If prolonged, it can lead to depression.

Sadness is expressed in various ways including:

- Crying

- Withdrawal from people

- Lethargy

- Quietness

- Dampened mood

Depending on the root cause, people can be assisted to cope with its severity to not sink into deeper complications like depression. Also, this emotion can be prolonged resulting in negative thoughts, if not well-managed.

**Fear**

Fear is one of the most powerful emotions and an important role in survival. When something causes you to fear, you are likely to develop a fight-or-flight response. All of a sudden, you become tense, your respiration and heartbeat increase, your sensory organs become alert, prompting your whole self to either fight back or run from danger. This response can cause you to do the unplanned in a way you cannot explain.

This kind of emotion can be expressed as follows:

- Facial expression: widening the eyes, opening your mouth, pulled back chin

- Action: run, fight back, and hide

- Physiological reaction: accelerated heartbeat, breathing heavily, panting

Different people express themselves differently in incidents of fear. Some people can become numb and even collapse in incidents of fear depending on the cause. For instance, a snake's sight may cause one to run, another to fight back, and another to become numb and motionless.

Fear can also result from thought regarding a potential danger, resulting in anxiety not knowing what exactly to expect.

Some other individuals love attempting fearful ventures, like extreme sports ventured by people who enjoy the feeling of attempting fearful things.

If consistently exposed to a fearful situation, it could lead to familiarity hence reducing the feeling of anxiety and fear. An example would be one who fears hearing gunshots. If they move near a barrack where gunshots from training soldiers are the order of the day, then gunshots' fear reduces with time.

**Disgust**

It can be displayed in the following ways:

· Turning your face away from the scene of disgust

· A physical reaction like vomiting

· A facial expression like closing eyes and wrinkling your nose

Disgust can be brought about by an unpleasant sight, smell, or taste. Food that has gone stale can cause a disgusting emotional reaction.

Other things that may trigger a disgusting emotion include decomposing body, rot, blood, untreated wound, and poor hygiene. The sight of immoral actions can also be disgusting.

**Anger**

Anger is also a major powerful emotion characterized by feelings of frustrations, agitation, hostility, and antagonism. Same as fear, anger can cause body fight-or-flight response to respond promptly. When feelings generate emotions of anger in you, you are likely to arise to fight back or defend yourself.

It is normally displayed through:

· Facial expression: glaring or frowning

· Body language: staring strongly at the source or turning away from the source

· Voice tone: yelling or speaking gruffly

· Physiological response: turning face color, sweating, shaking

· Aggressiveness: throwing objects, kicking, hitting

Most of the time, anger is presumed as a negative emotional reaction. Still, it can be constructive because it helps one express themselves in full, expel all the stored pain from within, and clarify your dissatisfaction with anger. Expressed anger hits the 'enough' button, and the situation has to be addressed.

However, anger can become uncontrollable leading to an unhealthy, dangerous, and harmful way of expression. For example, the aggregated can hit the other with an object leading to injury or even death. This is where uncontrolled anger turns to violence, abuse, and aggression.

Some health conditions in individuals can lead to uncontrolled anger when provoked. Such cases should be handled soberly, bearing in mind that it could run out of hand leading to unprecedented events.

Due to uncontrolled anger, some people have resulted in having diseases like coronary heart disease and diabetes, while others have found themselves in behaviors like smoking, alcoholism, and aggressive driving.

## Surprise

This emotion is normally brief. It is a physiological startle response resulting from an unexpected response. This kind of emotion can be negative, positive, or neutral. Example of a negative surprise could be arriving home and finding your pet dead, whereas a pleasant surprise could be an award from your boss for a well-done job.

It is characterized by:

- Facial expressions: raising eyebrows and opening the mouth
- Physical response: jumping up and down
- Verbal reactions: gasping, screaming, and yelling

Surprise emotion can also trigger a fight-or-flight response. There is a burst of adrenaline that causes the body to either flee or fight.

Surprise moments tend to linger more in the mind standing out in memory. Surprise news can get hold of people attention, and that's why newsmakers are more inclined to breaking news.

## Other Significant Types of Emotions

Other significant types of emotions that may not necessarily trigger expressions include:

- Amusement
- Shame
- Contentment
- Satisfaction
- Excitement

- Guilt
- Contempt
- Pride in achievement
- Embarrassment
- Relief

**Advantages of Emotions**

Emotions have three components, namely:

- Subjective (experience)
- Physiological (body reaction)
- Expressive (behavior response)

1.      Motivate to take action. Let's take for example when one is about to do a final exam that determines whether they step up or re-sit, there is a definite feeling of anxiety. The most emotional response will be to study. The motivation to study will outdo the anxiety to ensure you stand out with good grades.

Naturally, everyone will strive to engage in activities that bring positive emotions and avoiding those that are likely to trigger negative emotions.

2.      Boost our survival tactics and help us avoid danger. Charles Darwin believed emotions drive both humans and animals to manage and reproduce. Anger drives to confrontation, fear may cause us to move to safety areas, and love may cause us to look out for our mates for reproduction purposes.

Emotions are adaptive drivers taking us to a place of action that guarantees survival and success.

3.      Help in making decisions. Our emotions are major influencers in our decision making, right from what we take for breakfast to the leaders we choose during political elections.

Even though logic, rationality, and statics are key factors in making decisions our emotions determine the final move. Emotional intelligence has been proven to play a major role in our decision making.

4.        You are understood through your emotions. You should not be afraid to express yourself through your emotions. You can express your emotions through body language such as facial expressions of whatever emotions you are going through.

You can also express your emotions verbally, hence your listener will know your position on a particular issue and be advised how to react or help.

5.        Through emotions, you can understand others. Just as expressing our own emotions can help convey valuable information to others, likewise, we can understand others through the emotions of their display. It's important to be able to interpret and respond to others through the emotions they display. This enhances effective communication in dealing with different people as you consider their predicaments through their emotional expressions.

Charles Darwin, an early scientific researcher on emotions, indicates emotional display can save anyone from impending danger. For example, a spitting and hissing animal indicate that it's angry and possibly defensive, so the best thing is to back off and avoid it.

Understanding others through their emotional display will help us know how to respond calmly and amicably.

**The Significance Of Both Positive And Negative Emotions To Daily Life**

Some of the common positive emotions may include:

- Awe
- Serenity
- Happiness
- Amusement
- Interest
- Contentment
- Satisfaction
- Joy
- Love

Negative emotions include:

- Annoyance
- Melancholy
- Loneliness
- Rage
- Sadness
- Disgust
- Anger
- Fear

Both positive and negative emotions happen and for a good reason. For example:

- Disgust – we can reject unhealthy stuff.
- Trust – you can connect with genuine people.
- Sadness – you get to connect with our loved ones.
- Joy – it reminds us of what is important.
- Surprise – have a focus on new situations.
- Anticipation – you can look forward and plan.
- Fear – it protects us from anger.
- Anger – it enables us to fight against problems.

Unpleasant negative emotions are also important in our lives. Some seemingly positive emotions can be a major contributor to stress. For example:

- Planning for a wedding
- House moving (exiting at the same time stressing)
- Having a baby
- Starting on a new job

The above activities are positive and exciting but can bring negative emotions with them; hence both positive and negative emotions are inevitable.

# Chapter 3:   Building Solid Relationships

Emotions are a tricky subject because it involves matters in which people tend to assess their emotions quickly without knowing its actual meaning. Frequently, terminology about emotion is used incorrectly, or it is used so that it has been stripped of its real meaning. We may say that certain people are emotional, but it is not clear what that means. Even the person who uses the term emotional might be using it differently than how the person hearing it interprets it. Because emotional intelligence involves interactions, it is easy for emotional intelligence to be hindered because people use improper terminology or allow themselves to be misled by terms that have acquired a negative connotation.

Typically, when someone is described as emotional, this is intended to be taken in a negative light. Emotional people are often regarded as impulsive, difficult to talk to, difficult to work with, unscientific, irrational, loud, or resistant to being spoken to. But this characterization is based on assumptions about emotional people. Indeed, labeling someone as emotional is a simple and almost devious way to neutralize and invalidate someone by immediately labeling them as something they may or may not.

Words have power and in using words incorrectly and communicating them to people, we allow those words to become a part of that person because others will associate that person with those words that we have chosen to label them with. In labeling someone emotional, we have now doomed them to being interpreted in a specific light by others that they will be interacting with. This prevents them from being able to build social relationships and sustain them in a way that is healthy and beneficial for both.

Building social relationships is the end goal of emotional intelligence and highly emotionally intelligent people have been shown to have better social relationships with others. This leads to highly emotionally intelligent people being more successful in objective measures of success. "Emotional" people are thought to be better at relationships, but this is because "emotional" people are considered to think about emotions more than others do.

This perception has to do with the idea that thinking about emotions too much is something negative. These dysfunctional perceptions have led to some people eschewing in any emotion, while others have taken the opposite side and have become advocates for emotion and emotional thinking. But this is a downward spiral that results from terminology not being used appropriately in emotion. Showing compassion for someone is a sign that you feel emotion. All religions are infused with emotional feeling and people become better friends, better family members, and better lovers because they care.

Emotion is the basis for meaningful social relationships. Having emotions does not mean that you are bogged down by them, which is how some characterize it. By rejecting emotion or mischaracterizing emotion, we create a society where people either have distorted emotions because they do not understand them correctly or they feel no emotion at all because they have been taught to be wary of emotion based on misconceptions about emotion.

An easy way to think about emotion as the basis for building relationships is by thinking about how we relate to one another. When you engage in an act that is beneficial to someone other than yourself, you show emotion. Perhaps it is part of your spiritual or religious belief to engage in acts that show charity or kindness towards others. Perhaps you have donated clothes to a charitable organization or have assisted at a soup kitchen. These are all ways that you show care and concern for others.

Caring, concern, worry — these are all feelings that fall along the spectrum with sadness, anger, guilt, disappointment, hope, and all the other feelings that are part of being human. These are things that people should not run from but should embrace as they are essential to partaking in social relationships with others.

Suffice it to say that research proposes that highly emotionally intelligent people have better relationships and more successful group interactions than people who do not demonstrate emotional intelligence. Of course, these benefits stem from all aspects of emotional intelligence. People who have empathy, have better self-regulation skills, or demonstrate compassion will generally be liked and valued by their peers compared to those who are not.

One of the goals of this is not to approach emotion from the standpoint of two camps: those in favor of emotional thinking and those against it. This dichotomy approaches the subject from a distorted standpoint as it does not accept that feeling emotions are a normal part of being human. Indeed, lacking emotion or irregularly demonstrating emotion is a criterion for some psychiatric conditions in the Diagnostic and Statistical Manual. The goal of this is not therefore to lead you to see this subject from the standpoint of being an "emotional person" or an "unemotional (or rational) person." We all feel emotions and we need to claim them.

By understanding how having emotions ties into the many aspects of emotional intelligence, we can healthily approach the subject. Some of the stigma that comes from so-called emotional people is that people labeled as emotional may not engage in the associated steps of understanding other people's emotions, self-regulation, and empathy. This was touched on in the discussion of narcissism. Still, those who healthily embrace their emotions also embrace others' emotions and know how to regulate their emotions if they begin to get in the way of social interactions.

Social relationships, therefore, require that all the components of emotional intelligence be used effectively. Indeed, the topic of healthy social relationships helps tie together the power of emotional intelligence as a tool as it does not focus merely on one area. To build and maintain social relationships, an individual must:

- Demonstrate compassion and tolerance for others
- Have empathy
- Assess one's emotions and the emotions of others
- Understand the emotions of others
- Make an effort to relate to others
- Regulate one's own emotions

Social relationships are complex, whether they are romantic in nature, friendships, or employer-employee relationships. By tying together all aspects of emotional intelligence, men and women can create and maintain important relationships. This is not just true of individuals in the workplace. Research has shown clearly that going through the different intelligences that comprise emotional intelligence is important for adults in their relationships and children in the school setting.

**Non-Verbal Communication**

Non-verbal communication is essential to social interactions in humans. Although human beings do have the capability of producing speech, the cues that we send that do not involve words are just as important in conveying our feelings, desires, and intentions as the words that we say. Non-verbal communication is almost a form of mind-reading, which can be both positive and negative. By communicating without words, sometimes we can express how we feel more accurately and more deeply. As a song from the 90s goes: "Words are meaningless, especially sentences." It is not always easy to describe what we are feeling with words.

Non-verbal communication is sometimes overlooked because everyone does it so it is easy to take it for granted. Overlooked or not, non-verbal communication is important as it allows to be cued in to what we are feeling or thinking. Recall that empathy and emotional intelligence, in general, requires that the other person be able to gauge our emotions and experiences accurately. This means that non-verbal communication comprises a set of non-verbal cues that others will use to be able to gauge what we feel accurately.

This is important because it means that we must be keyed in the non-verbal cues of others and our cues that we are sending. This is distinct from the self-regulation that is part and parcel of emotional intelligence, but there are some similarities. Sometimes it may be important to curtail our negative cues or cues that may push people away even if they reflect how we feel. Although this may seem to some like dishonesty, it is just a recognition that interactions with others are important and that sometimes we have to coordinate and control our cues to be able to interact with others. The assumption here is that others will be engaging in a similar dance of regulation of non-verbal cues, which is all a part of normal human interaction.

The question then becomes what the non-verbal cues are that others are responding to. There are many gestures, movements, postures, and other things that we do as people to indicate what we are feeling internally. Some of these are gestures that naturally crop up due to our internal state, like the furrowed brow that indicates worry. In contrast, others are acquired postures that we pick up sometimes without knowing, like placing your hands on your hips when you are irritated, angry, or in a hurry.

No matter where our gestures originate, it is important to be conscious of them so that we can think about how others may interpret our gestures. Although the argument can be made that we should not alter these non-verbal cues as they accurately reflect how we feel, sometimes it is necessary to control our own emotions (or indications of our emotion) as part of showing sympathy or empathy others.

Therefore, being conscious of our non-verbal cues becomes an essential part of the social interactions that we have with others. People who frequently show non-verbal cues that indicate negative or frustrated emotions will likely be perceived more negatively by people than those whose gestures are more positive. Although everyone goes through trying times and everyone naturally feels anger, sadness, frustration, tiredness, and the like, paying attention to our social cues can help us get along better with others and have more fruitful outcomes from our interactions.

Although most people will be acquainted with the sorts of non-verbal cues that indicate our internal emotional state, it may be helpful to some people to review them here. Some of these non-verbal cues include:

- Body position
- Facial expression
- Hand position
- Yawning
- Laughter
- Hands on hips
- Speed of speech
- Tapping of the foot
- Vocal Tone
- Looking away or not making eye contact

By paying attention to the cues listed above, you can effectively show sympathy, have empathy, and set yourself on the path towards becoming a highly emotionally intelligent individual.

# Chapter 4:  Overcoming Negativity

Mental preparation is the key to overcoming negativity.

Some of the most successful people in the world start their day every morning by mentally preparing themselves for the day.

They meditate, recite their goals to themselves, use positive affirmations ,or even listen to motivational podcasts on their phones or other mobile devices.

Essentially, they do whatever it takes to prepare their minds to focus on blocking out and minimizing the impact of any kind of negativity they are going to encounter.

Life is going to put you through a countless emotions. You're going to experience everything from excitement ,fear, stress, pressure, passion, determination and more.

There is a thing that will help you get through it all and come out triumphant on the other side–overcoming negativity.

## •    Think About It

When a negative thought pops into our heads, we don't stop to think enough if this is a thought that should be taken seriously.

Is there a cause for alarm? Or could be perhaps be exaggerating the thought in our minds, making it sound worse than what it is.

External factors trigger some negative thoughts and emotions.

You might be tired, hungry, exhausted, overworked or already feeling tense at the time of the negative thought, which probably aggravated the situation.

When you're already not in the best frame of mind, a small issue can seem worse than what it is.

The next period you find yourself dwelling on a negative thought, stop and think about it for a minute and ask yourself if it's justified.

- **Have an Action Plan**

There are always going to be unpleasant challenges. We can't run away from it, even if we wanted to.

But viewing those challenges from a negative perspective is only going to make things much worse for you.

On the other hand, having a plan of action about what you can do to manage the unexpected un-pleasantries that life may occasionally throw your way will keep you moving forward and no longer be held back despite the negativity that you feel.

When Plan A fails, have a Plan B, a Plan C, and as many back-up plans as you need.

Be as adaptable and fluid as water, ever ready to twist and turn to continue forging a path forward, because that's the only way to go forward.

Having a plan instead of having no plan at all, helps you manage the way you feel.

- Think About What's Helpful

Whenever you've experienced a setback, the last thing you might be thinking about is how this situation is helpful to you.

As bleak or negative as a situation may be, one trick mentally tough individuals use to help them maintain their optimism is to think about what helpful lesson they can take away from the setbacks they experienced.

It could be one lesson, it could be two, it could be as many lessons as you'd like.

No matter how bad things seem, there's always a silver lining, it's up to you to find it by asking yourself the right questions.

Questions like what have I learned from this experience? What can I do to make it better moving forward? What's one positive takeaway from this situation?

- **Observe Your Surroundings**

Your environment has an enormous impact on the way that you feel. The place you spend most of your time is going to weigh on your mind subconsciously. You may not be actively thinking about your surroundings, but it's there in the back of your mind.

If you find it hard to remain positive throughout the day, do a quick scan of your surroundings and observe the negativity sources.

Your cluttered workstation? The toxic colleague who is constantly complaining and talking negatively about other colleagues behind their back?

Maybe that pile of paperwork you've been postponing for a while now and haven't gotten around to doing yet.

Once you've identified a potential source, ask yourself what you can do to rectify the problem.

Can the source be removed entirely? If it can't what else could you do to spend less time around this negative source in a week?

- **Stop Feeding into Your Thoughts**

Feeding into your negative thoughts is only going to fuel it to become even more out of control.

A thought may start small, but the more you continue to obsess and dwell over the matter, the bigger that thought eventually seems to become.

The expression making a mountain out of a molehill is completely applicable to this situation.

We sometimes build up our fears so much in our minds that they seem disastrous until we eventually face them and come to realize it wasn't so bad after all.

- **Find Inspiration Daily**

The perfect way to cultivate a positive mindset and minimize negativity is to wake up each morning and make the first thing that you see something that is going to inspire you.

Pick a quote or a saying, stick pictures of inspirational quotes on your mirrors, in your cubicle at work, a note on your phone, make it your wallpaper on your computer, and just surround yourself with it so it's hard to miss.

Starting on a positive note will help set the tone for the rest of the day, so wake up each morning and let positivity be the first and dominant feeling that helps to start your day right.

Every day is another chance, another opportunity to begin anew, and it is what you do today - not what has happened in the past - that matters most.

- **Cultivate Positive Dialogue**

We've established by now just how powerful your thoughts can be. If your thoughts can influence negativity, they also have that same power to do the opposite.

You need to start tapping into that force and begin creating a more optimistic mindset.

You must push every negative thought you have about yourself out of your mind and start replacing it with something positive instead.

Imagine your negative thoughts as physical boulders in front of you, and you need to forcefully push those out of your mind and clear the path for newer, better things.

For every negative thought that you find yourself thinking, stop and immediately replace that thought with a positive one.

- **Reshape Your Failure Perspective**

Instead of thinking about them as failures, see them as lessons instead.

They're not failures, they're learning experiences that teach you what not to do, and what needs improvement.

We are constantly learning something new, always growing and developing into a better version of yourself.

Nobody can do everything perfectly, or always get it from the first go without taking a few stumbles along the way.

Every successful person out there today that has made their mark and becomes a household name didn't get to where they are without taking a few tumbles and stumbles along the way.

They too made plenty of mistakes before they got to the pinnacle of success.

Change your mind set by changing the way you see these failures, don't focus on how you failed but instead, start thinking about how you can improve next time or what you can do differently.

- **Keep Your Company Positive**

Negative people will only weigh you down. They'll drain you of energy, become a mental and emotional burden that you don't need.

When you attach yourself to people who think positive, you'll slowly adapt the way you think to emulate them as their wisdom, outlook, stories, and affirmations slowly seep into your way of thinking.

Examine the people in your life right now, and if any individuals

in it are toxic with their negative outlook, it's time to start distancing yourself from them.

### How To Overcome Negativity

You need to believe in yourself. Believe that you are stronger than you give yourself credit for, believe that you deserve to have a better, happier life.

You'll never truly achieve the level of positive mindset you hope for if you still have those nagging thoughts at the back of your mind that make you doubt yourself every step of the way.

Whenever you feel your emotions receiving the better of you, stop and take a breath.

Focusing on your breathing will help you shift your focus and mind from feeling anxious, nervous, scared or angry to calm, steadiness and peace.

By believing you can achieve it, you've already put yourself one step closer to making it happen for real.

# Chapter 5:    Importance of Empathy

Empathy plays a dominant role in our society's ability to function, promoting our needs, sharing experiences, and desires among one another. Our neural networks are set up to connect with others' neural systems to both see and comprehend their feelings and separate them from our own. This makes it possible for people to live with each other without feeling that someone is in control.

Empathy is vital as it helps us comprehend and understand the feelings of others, and what they are going through, so that we can be able to respond appropriately to the situation at hand. To a greater extent, empathy has been associated with the social behaviors. There is plenty of research supporting this argument. Thus, the higher the degree of empathy a person feels, the more they tend to help others. Notably, an empath can also control actions or even go to the extent of curtailing immoral behavior. For example, someone who sees a car accident and is overwhelmed by emotions upon witnessing the victims in severe pain, might be far more inclined to help the victims or call for help.

Additionally, having strong empathetic feelings can also lead to negative effects. When a person demonstrates strong feelings toward people or causes, negative emotions may be stirred in others due to their insecurities. A perfect example of this can be seen in the way charlatans such as so-called fortune tellers exploit the insecurities of individuals. As a result, they may be able to trick empaths into actually believing that the end of the world is upon us and so forth.

Interestingly, people with a more pronounced psychopathic trait are said to show a more pragmatic response to events where there are moral dilemmas, such as the "footbridge dilemma". In this thought experiment, the conductor of a runaway train has to make a choice: since the train has no breaks it is heading toward five people crossing the tracks. Alternatively, the conductor may switch tracks and hit only one. Thus, the dilemma lies in whether you choose to kill one or kill all five people crossing the street. Hence, a pragmatic approach would lead to killing the least number of people whereas an empathetic approach would lead to killing none.

## Measuring Empathy

Quite often, a self-report questionnaire is used in measuring empathy. This is in the Interpersonal Reactivity Index (IRI) or the Questionnaire for Cognitive and Affective Empathy (QCAE). In measuring empathy, the person is asked to indicate how much they accept the statements that are set to help measure the different types of empathy that one might be having.

One will find statements like "It affects me very much when one of my friends is upset," which QCAE test uses to measure empathy. QCAE plays a key role in identifying cognitive empathy by the use of statements the likes of "I try to look at everybody's side of a disagreement before I make a decision."

With this method, it was discovered that people scoring higher on affective empathy have more grey matter. Grey matter is said to be a collection of nerve cells in the anterior insula, an area of the brain.

This zone is regularly associated with directing positive and negative feelings by coordinating external stimuli, such as seeing an auto crash - with automatic and programmed sensations. Likewise, individuals utilizing this strategy gauging compassion have found that high scorers of sympathy had a progressively dark issue in the dorsomedial prefrontal cortex.

The activation of this particular area occurs when there are more cognitive processes; this includes the Theory of the Mind. As stated earlier, this theory calls for the individual to understand the beliefs, intentions and motivations that drive them. As a result, the individual is then able to immerse themselves in the mindset of others fully.

## Can Humans Lack Empathy?

Several cases have proven that not all humans have empathy. For instance, walking down Minnesota, you bump into a homeless person shivering in the cold. You will notice that few people will express sympathy or compassion for the homeless person. There are many cases in which passersby express outright hostility towards such people. So, what could be the cause of expressing what seems to be selective empathy? Various elements come to mind: how we see the other individual, how we characterize their actions, what we attribute their misfortunes to, and our past encounters and desires. These all become an integral factor in our ability to express or repress empathy.

Furthermore, the two main things that contribute to experiencing empathy are socialization and genetics. And while the "nature vs. nurture" debate is far from being conclusively settled, the fact of the matter is that our preconceived notions tend to influence the way we act and react when confronted with a situation that requires us to express compassion in a fellow human being.

Here are the top reasons why we sometimes lack empathy:

a) We fall victim to cognitive biases

In this factor, our cognitive biases, that is, our judgments, lead us to pin the misfortunes on an individual on themselves. We tend to attribute their pain and suffering to their shortcomings instead of being compassionate and attempting to aid the victim whenever possible. These biases can be the result of societal and cultural perceptions.

b) We dehumanize victims

Quite often, we tend to view victims as people who are different from us. For example, the common "that will never happen to me" concept creates a barrier that separates us from our fellows. In this regard, we not only dehumanize the victim, but we don't necessarily assume that they are in pain and suffering. This is generally when victims are viewed as number and statistics rather the flesh and blood beings who suffer and experience sorrow.

c) We blame victims

This is one of the most common responses when analyzing someone's misfortunes. We tend to see them as victims of their consequences. And while there are situations in which that is true, the fact of the matter is that a true empath does not care how a person got to be in their situation. All they care about is how to help the victim feel better or even solve the issue they are in.

True empaths can filter out logic and reason insofar as assigning blame and responsibility and looking at the reality of what others are experiencing. So, even if it is the victim's fault, it doesn't matter. What matters is that the person needs help. That means that the rest can be sorted out later on.

Moreover, blaming a person's misfortunes on themselves tends to take away any responsibility from others. That is, if the victim is responsible for their lot, then they should be the ones to solve their problem. As such, why are they asking for help if they were the ones who caused the problem in the first place? Such attitudes create a significant barrier for empathy.

## Can Empathy Be Selective?

It is good to note that we don't generally feel empathy for the people who are directly responsible for their actions in such times. The brain reacts very differently when we see people suffering from what we perceive to be an injustice. However, if we feel that their pain is justified, the brain nullifies empathy.

These

perceptions also extend to ethnic and social groups. We see the suffering of people from varying social groups in a very different light. For example, the poor have little to no empathy for the rich; the rich may view the poor solely responsible for their lot. Thus, empathy tends to become skewed in one direction or another.

Consequently, it is encouraged to practice empathy regardless of social class or ethnicity. While this is hard to do, it is a skill which can be practiced and developed over time. Nevertheless, the true empath will not find it difficult to identify with others.

## Determining If You Are An Empath

Here is a simple trial that can help you define if you are an empath or not. You can go through it, giving a simple "yes" or "no" answer to each question.

- Have I in any time been labeled as sensitive, introvert, or shy?
- Do I get anxious or overwhelmed frequently?
- Do fights, yelling, and arguments often make me ill?
- Do I often have the feeling that I don't fit in?
- Do I find myself being drained by the crowds, and by that then do I mostly need my time alone to revive myself?
- Do odors, noise, or nonstop talkers get me overwhelmed?
- Do I have chemical sensitiveness or low tolerance for scratchy clothes?
- Do I prefer using my car when attending an event or going to a place to be free to leave earlier?
- Do I use food as my source to escape from stress?
- Do I feel afraid of being suffocated by relationship intimacy?
- Do I easily startle?
- Do I have a strong reaction to medications or caffeine?
- Do I have a low threshold for pain?
- Do I tend to be socially isolated?
- Do I get to absorb the stress, symptoms, and emotions of the other people?

- Am I mostly overwhelmed by doing several things at a go, and do I always prefer handling one thing at a go?
- Do I replenish myself generally?
- Do I need a long time to get better after being with tough people or energy vampires?
- Do I always feel being in a better place while in small cities than the big ones?
- Do I always prefer having one on one interaction and small groups and not the large gathering?

You can now try to know who you are by calculating your results.

- If you agreed to at least five of the questions, then you are partly an empath.
- If you agreed to at least ten questions, you are at a moderate level.
- If you agreed to eleven or fifteen questions, you are a strong empath with strong tendencies.
- If you have agreed to more than fifteen questions, then it's without a doubt that you are a full-blown empath.

The determination of your degree of an empath is important as it will make it easy for you to clarify the types of needs and the type of strategy you will need to adapt in a bit to meet them. With the determination, then you will be able to find a comfort zone in your life.

# Chapter 6: Self-Awareness

Self-awareness describes a heightened state of understanding that helps you become closer with yourself on a deeper level. You begin to see the obstacles that stand in your way and what you can do to overcome them. By living a life of progress and development, you can feel proud and confident in your journey. By deciding which parts of your personality you want to shine, you can effectively create the life you want to live.

## Signs Of Low Self-Esteem

People who live with low self-esteem usually develop it years before they realize what is going on. Some may still be struggling from problems they had in their adolescence. Other people may begin struggling with their self-esteem in adulthood, as they try to build a life that they can appreciate. Regardless of when feelings of low self-esteem begin, the first step is identifying that you are struggling.

Here are the common signs of low self-esteem:

- Constantly thinking negative thoughts about yourself
- Focusing heavily on your flaws and weaknesses, without the intent of inspiring change or fixing a problem
- Difficulty handling stressful situations
- Fear of failure
- Difficulty accepting compliments or positive feedback
- A need to have the approval or reassurance of others
- A need to establish social status or show of possessions to seem more appealing to others
- Difficulty trying new things

- Behaviors like promiscuity, drinking, using drugs, and acting impulsively

If you recognized at least 3 of the behaviors above, you may struggle with self-esteem. You can also consider your overall feelings about yourself. If you feel confident in yourself and feel that you have a purpose, you probably have good self-esteem. However, if you are unsure of your purpose in life, you might be struggling with self-love.

## Signs Of Low Self-Confidence

Lack of confidence can drastically impact your life. It affects the people you are comfortable approaching and the situations that you put yourself in. There are many signs of low self-confidence, including:

- You cannot leave the house without doing your hair and makeup or otherwise priming yourself
- You back down in disagreements to avoid conflict
- You use your phone frequently in social situations
- You are indecisive, even when making simple decisions like where to eat
- You have trouble sharing your opinion with others
- You have trouble accepting constructive criticism
- You have poor posture
- You compare yourself with others
- You have trouble accepting compliments
- You give up on goals easily and have trouble trying new things

If you have 4-5 of these characteristics, you may struggle with self-confidence. Remember that confidence can be situational. You may feel confident at work, for example, but struggle in social situations.

## Becoming Self-Aware

Self-awareness is something that occurs in levels. Studies show that a person generally becomes aware of themselves and how they differentiate from the people around them beginning around age 18 months. For children, a heightened state of self-awareness is developed by age 4 or 5. At this time, they understand their movements in a mirror are their own and they can identify themselves in pictures and videos. There is also an understanding that they exist from the perspective of others as well. This self-awareness continues through life, but it is the way that it is used that affects the role that being self-aware has in our lives.

## Public Vs. Personal Self-Awareness

People eventually develop two types of self-awareness. The first type is public self-awareness, which is a heightened awareness of how other people perceive you. Public self-awareness is the reason people make certain decisions in public to go along with social norms. It is most common in times when people are the center of attention, such as when they are telling a story to their friends or giving a presentation at work.

When people focus too much on adhering to societal norms, it can cause anxiety or distress. They may worry too much about how people will respond to them, so they hang back in social situations and avoid trying new things because they are afraid of how they react. When you have too much public self-awareness, you can question your own decisions and actions.

Private self-awareness describes the way that you are aware of yourself. It is not usually physical aspects since it describes an internal and personal awareness. It may be the physical symptoms like butterflies in your stomach when you see someone you are attracted to or the panic that sets in when you realize you have not studied for your test. Even though nobody around you can tell that your palms are sweating (unless they are physically shaking your hand), you are personally aware of your nervousness.

## How To Use Personal And Public Awareness

The goal of self-awareness is not to make yourself self-conscious. You should not put yourself in a position where you are incredibly anxious or questioning your decisions. Be aware of everything. Be aware of your strengths and weaknesses. Be aware of those times that you have succeeded in tough situations and the mistakes that have taught you lessons. When considering public awareness, be aware of how people's perceptions of you affect your relationship and the offered opportunities.

The proper way to use self-awareness is to use it in a way that better yourself. Someone who does not share their ideas in the office because they are afraid of others' judgment will miss out on opportunities like leading a project or taking on a high-profile client. Their boss perceives them as someone who does not have innovative ideas or lacks self-confidence and thus gives the more

45

important roles in the organization to someone they think is more capable of handling the situation.

As you become aware of the strengths and weaknesses, you can learn to harness those strengths to help build on useful skills. You also learn which areas you can improve in. Another benefit is better quality relationships. When you are aware of personal relationships and how the other person feels about you, you gain insight into making the relationship better. For example, someone may be aware that their mom is sad at the end of their visits. This perception might cause them to ask her what is wrong—she just might be sad because they don't visit often, and she knows she won't see them for a while.

Finally, becoming self-aware helps you learn how to nurture yourself. Your goals become clearer as you realize the things that make you happy and fill you with purpose. The benefit of certain relationships in your life will also become clearer. You'll learn which relationships to give your energy and attention to, as well as which relationships are bringing you further from your life's path or that harm your life. Overall, you'll have a better insight into what you need to do to make your goals a reality.

**Increasing Self-Awareness With Meditation**

Meditation is often grouped with spiritual habits or religion. However, meditating regularly does not have to be about religion. It is about discipline. Meditation is a form of mental discipline that quiets the busy chatter many people have in their mind. Think back to the last time that you were eating or taking a shower. Do you spend your lunch break at work enjoying your food and taking a much-needed break so your mind can refresh? Or are you thinking about the things you want to finish before going home for the night? Are you stressing over life when you are in the shower? Or are you taking the time to enjoy the water's warmth after a tiring day and the pleasant feeling of getting clean?

The average person lives a busy life. It is generally believed that if you want to be successful, you have to stay busy. There is always something else to be done and it is not uncommon to spend time that should be spent relaxing worrying about those unfinished things. This is the reality of life for many people, but it creates an unhappy existence. When you do not give yourself the time to slow down and reflect on your life, you are not giving yourself the time to prepare yourself for self-improvement. Then, you may find yourself stuck in the same pattern without having a specific goal all through your life.

## Benefits Of Meditation For Self-Awareness

Meditation is often referred to as 'the path to enlightenment'. Self-aware people know themselves on a deeper level and this allows them to shape their life. The goal with this meditation, however, does not have to be religious. When you meditate for self-reflection, you are looking within to understand yourself because you are your life's creator. You are the only person who can choose if you keep working a dead-end job or take the steps to further your dreams. You are the only person who can choose if you want to spend the rest of your life with the person you are dating or pulling you away from your life's path. Here's a look at how self-reflective meditation can change your life.

- Building a foundation of truth- People do not always know who they are at their core. Other times, they may have strayed so far from their beliefs that they have lost the meaning of what they were. Meditation reflection helps you see those areas where you have deviated from your value system.

- Better use of talent- Sometimes, we end up pushed down life's path with little thought to what we are good at. Consider someone who has an art degree from college—but works in a factory because it was the first open position they found after graduating college. Even though they are talented as artists, they are always tired from work and don't work to advance that talent. They get stuck in this job even though they despise it and eventually end up staying on because of their loyalty. However, they are miserable with their lives and their passions are going to waste. When you reflect on things that make you happy, it allows you to see the talents that you have tucked away. By reflecting on these strengths, you can find the inspiration to grow them and use them in a way that benefits your life.

- Improved goal-mindedness- When you do not set goals for yourself, you move through life aimlessly and without direction. There is no pressure for doing something, so it is easy to say you will start 'tomorrow' or 'next month'. If you do not hold yourself to it, however, you will never see results. Reflection gives you time to think about your goals and the path to achieving them. It also lets you set time aside to consider your accountability in meeting your goals and whether you are actively trying to reach them.

# Chapter 7:    Responses to Your Emotinal Triggers

Feelings, especially intense feelings, can often be autonomous, which means they are automatic and subconscious, developing as the result of an external force or trigger. If someone cuts you off in traffic, for example, the anger that bubbles up in your gut is generated without conscious thought or intent.

To take control of our emotional selves, we must learn to be aware of our emotional triggers and our natural responses to those triggers. The perfect way to do this is to practice mindfulness.

## What Is Mindfulness?

Sometimes, intense negative emotion causes us to become disconnected or detached, moving through daily life without engaging with our emotions and experiences. This feeling of being disconnected is very common in people struggling with depression and high anxiety or stress. To combat this emotional distress, we must learn to become more present within our lives, live with our eyes open to what's going on around us, and impact our emotional well-being. To put things as simply as possible, we need to turn off "auto-pilot" and begin to be aware of how we feel and why.

As emotional beings, we are naturally mindful. Still, it can be difficult to be fully present when dealing with high anxiety or anger or other negative emotions. When we practice mindfulness, we force ourselves to face these emotions, consider them and learn to understand them. We can cultivate mindfulness through a variety of techniques, the most common and widely practiced being meditation.

## What Is Meditation?

Meditation is an excellent relaxation technique that also helps us connect with our inner truths. Meditation aims to quiet the mind and body, remove insignificant thoughts, and develop inner balance by interacting with our emotional selves without the constant external and internal chatter. Meditation itself is a rather simple activity, but calming the body and mind is easier said than done. By introducing meditation into your routine, you will get better and better at it, and you will begin to crave the positive and peaceful feelings it can bring out.

## How Does Meditation Promote Mindfulness?

When we meditate, we steer our awareness away from the external and turn it inwards, paying attention to what the body and mind are doing without life's external noise. Meditation promotes relaxation, which relieves the body of stress and stress hormones and allows it to function more easily. When the body is less stressed, there are fewer physical distractions from what is going on in the mind. When we are meditating, we are naturally more aware of our thoughts and emotions, and we are open to the insights we have within ourselves.

## How Do I Meditate?

When I first read about meditation's possible benefits, I was hesitant to try it, mostly because, well, what if I was doing it wrong? It turns out, I didn't have anything to worry about, because there is no right or wrong way to meditate. It all depends on what works best for you and what is most comfortable. If you don't know where to begin, here's a step-by-step guide to meditation.

- Set an intention for today's practice. Your intention may simply be to practice meditation, especially at the beginning. As you become more accustomed to meditation, you may set a more specific intention before you begin, such as seeking intuition regarding a struggle in your life. If you choose to set a specific intention, begin with a question. How do I deal with ____? Ask yourself this question and see what answers you get.

- Find a quiet, comfortable place to sit. The most important thing is that you find a comfortable seat that will not strain your muscles. Cross your legs, or if this is not comfortable, spread them out in front of you to relax into the floor/couch/bed/comfy spot. If your hips do not like this position, try elevating your butt with a pillow or folded towel. This can relieve tension in the hips.

- Relax your body into an upright position. You don't want to strain your muscles; allow your body to relax into your spine's natural curvature. Relax your body from top to bottom, starting with the face. You can relax your face by focusing on relaxing your forehead and jaw muscles. Let your arms fall parallel to your body, and rest your hands on your legs. Work your way down until your body feels tension-free (or as tension-free as possible) and grounded into your seat.

- Close your eyes or focus on a single point. It is common to close one's eyes during meditation, but that can make it easier to fall asleep. If you do fall asleep, don't beat yourself up. It happens, especially when meditation is new. If you don't want to close your eyes, choose a spot in front of you to focus on. You may focus on a spot on the floor in front of you, light a candle, or set up a calming landscape poster.

- Take calming breaths and notice your breathing. It doesn't matter how you breathe as much as it matters that you pay attention to your breaths. Feel each inhale and exhale move through your body. Focusing on your breathing encourages mindfulness of the body and allows the mind the quiet.

- As thoughts enter your mind, allow them to pass through. When a thought comes up, you want to try to release it, let it flow out of your head as quickly as it flowed in. By emptying the mind, we allow our inner voice to be heard through intuitions. Your mind will probably wander, but that's okay. What you're trying to cultivate is an ability to be present at the moment and connect with yourself in a judgment-free environment.

- Consider setting a timer. Especially when you are first starting with meditation, you will probably have limited stamina. Begin with short, five-minute sessions, working up from there to spend longer and longer periods meditating. By setting a timer, you can avoid the distraction of how many seconds or minutes have passed and instead focus on your practice.

- Consider using a mantra. When you think about mediation, do you imagine a monk sitting cross-legged uttering "om" over and over? This is called a mantra, and you may choose to use one if your thoughts are particularly lively. Choose a neutral or positive word or phrase and repeat it throughout the exercise. You may say your mantra aloud or in your mind.

**Using Mindfulness To Recognize Your Emotional Triggers**

For the most part, our intense negative emotions manifest automatically due to some internal or external trigger. This could be a negative thought, a traumatic event, or even just an unexpected change. What triggers emotions in you will not necessarily trigger others, and what triggers emotions in others may not do the same for you. This is where mindfulness comes in. When you find yourself caught by the tide of negative emotion, try to identify what exactly caused you to feel this way. Here's a list of some possible triggers for common negative emotions:

Stress

- Change in the environment (a big move, a new job, etc.)
- Change in family life (marriage, divorce, a new baby, etc.)
- Changes in social life (discord among friends, someone moving away, etc.)
- Change in health (new or worsening illness, an injury, etc.)
- Change or increase in financial responsibilities (losing a job, etc.)
- Change in the workplace (tension among coworkers, getting fired, etc.)
- General disorder (a cluttered home, child and pet messes, etc.)

Anger

- Betrayal by a trusted person or entity
- Being disrespected, challenged, or insulted
- Being physically or emotionally threatened
- Being patronized or condescended to
- Being lied to/given misinformation

- The injustice done to you or others
- Discrimination/prejudice

Fear

- Threat of death
- Threat of injury or pain
- Loss of perceived safety/security
- Dark or unfamiliar environment
- Imagining a threatening event
- Reliving past fear or trauma
- Feeling exposed/vulnerable

Anxiety

- Anticipating failure or discomfort
- Feeling unprepared or insecure
- Feeling inadequate or worthless
- Negative self-talk/self-deprecation
- Upcoming event, performance, or challenge
- Social and familial conflict
- Remembering bad experiences
- Personal strain (due to finances, travel, etc.)

Sadness/Grief

- Major illness in a friend or loved one
- The death of a friend or loved one
- Temporary separation from loved ones
- Feeling rejected or unwanted
- A loss of identity or self-worth
- Anticipating future tragedy
- Disappointment in self or others
- Involuntary memories of loss or disappointment

Once we know what is triggering our emotional distress, we can begin to put together techniques and strategies to cope with it healthily.

## Using Mindfulness To Recognize Your Emotional Responses

To gain mastery over your emotions, you will need to practice recognizing how you respond to your emotional triggers. If you're angry at your significant other because of something that was said, consider how you're responding and what made you angry in the first place. Do you shut down and avoid the conflict? Do you explode into screams and rants? Practice recognizing how your body and mind respond to intense emotions, and consider which reactions are positive and negative.

## The Role Of Self-Talk

One of the most important aspects of mindfulness is being aware of how you talk to yourself. You must learn to pay attention to how you interact with yourself within your private thoughts because poor self-talk exacerbates poor emotional health. Self-talk is constant, and it can be easy to get in the habit of speaking to oneself from a place of judgment. We more readily notice our shortcomings than we do our skills, talents, and successes, and when we focus our self-talk around these negative things, we influence how we feel negatively.

Consider how you talk to yourself. Here's a list of common ways people engage in negative self-talk:

- Self-defamation (I look fat, I am stupid, I can't do anything right, etc.)
- Self-criticism over a past event (I should've done, should've said, etc.)
- Doubting own abilities (the ever destructive "I can't")
- Dismissing own abilities and good qualities
- Focusing on own perceived faults and failures
- Personalizing things that are out of our control
- Thinking in black and white (in terms of extremes)
- Assuming we know what the future holds

By practicing mindfulness, we can acknowledge the destructive ways we communicate with ourselves to be more empathetic and forgiving of our emotional struggles. Once you get in the habit of practicing mindfulness, you can begin to build coping strategies to remove your emotional triggers and change your responses to the triggers you can't get rid of. You may even begin to do this naturally once you are more aware of your triggers and reactions.

# Chapter 8: Emotional Intelligence In An Angry World

Anger is something that we all feel from time to time. But as a society, we're generally not very good at handling our anger. One cause why this happens is that we tend to think of anger as a negative emotion. The thing is, anger is a neutral emotion. It's what we do with it that makes it either positive or negative. Some people have done great things when faced with anger, righting the wrongs that they see, marched for good causes, and advocated for better things that they have been angry about. Other people, though, have done some pretty terrible things in a fit of rage. They've become aggressive, destructive, even violent, all examples of how anger can become negative when used for the wrong reasons. Anger is one of our core emotions as a human being, used to describe how we feel, and it helps us identify and connect with what is happening around us. What you do with anger is entirely up to you. It can be used to propel you positively, or propel you in the opposite direction too.

On its own, though, anger is neutral, but like most people, you've probably thought of anger in a negative context. Most people are either afraid of this emotion or try to deny the emotion altogether. It's easy to see why anger has developed an unpleasant reputation. In moments of anger, we make poor decisions. We lose all sense of rationale, and our emotional intelligence ceases to exist. All we feel is pure rage (in extreme cases), the blood pounding in our veins, and our muscles become tense and angry. Anger is a raw emotion that can lead you to do things you ordinarily would not do. Anger seems to hijack all our common sense and make it impossible to make good decisions when consumed by this emotion. All we end up doing is either hurting ourselves, the people around us, and feel full of regret with how badly the situation was handled.

## Understanding Your Anger

Different people would have different emotional triggers that set off this reaction, and there could be several factors that cause you to feel angry. Some examples of these triggers include:

- You feel powerless.
- You don't feel accomplished.
- You experience an unfair treatment against you or someone else.
- You've been lied to.
- You are ignored or mistreated.
- You think you're being neglected.
- You experience verbal or physical assault.
- You think your colleagues are not pulling their weight.
- You secretly resent having to take on more responsibility.
- You witness an injustice.
- You're disappointed.
- Promises are broken.
- Things don't go your way.

There is also the fact that some people generally have a shorter fuse than others do. Other possible reasons behind why you find yourself losing your temper more often than you should include:

Your Personality and Temperament- Competitive personalities tend to have shorter fuses because those with this personality type generally insist or demand that things go their way. We're not wired the same way. Some act quicker, while others need more time to process their next move. Some jump to action without thinking twice, while others need more time to ponder the consequences. Some people are more outgoing and adventurous; some are more laid back and introverted.

Your Role Models - Did you have parents or other family members who were quick to anger? Sometimes the cause of our short fuses is because the role models we had are what we can identify with. We don't know any other way because this is how we were raised. If one or both of your parents tended to be quick to anger, chances are you're likely to have that same tendency too. If that's the type of environment you grew up in, you're probably not going to see anything wrong with it until it's pointed out to you.

Mood Disorders - An undiagnosed personality disorder could trigger your short fuse without even realizing it. Bipolar disorder, depression, anxiety are all potential triggers because it won't take much to make you angry. If you suspect you may have any of these mood disorders, it is best that you seek professional help and don't leave it undiagnosed.

Higher Stress Levels - No surprises here that stress could be a cause for your short fuse. Being under a lot of pressure could lead to abrupt outbursts, temper tantrums, and irrational behavior. It is your body's way of reacting to the stress that you already feel.

Inability to Communicate Expressively - When you have a hard time making yourself understood or expressing yourself, it can often lead to a lot of feelings of frustration. Poor communication skills can lead to a lot of misunderstanding, which could lead to arguments which cause your temper to rise because you feel like your point is not getting across. Poor communication skills are yet another potential trigger for why you may have a shorter fuse than others.

Sleep Deprivation - A lack of sleep could also act as a potential trigger for a short fuse. Have you ever noticed how things seem much harder or require more effort when you're feeling tired and exhausted from lack of sleep? You feel cranky, irritable, and even the smallest of things seem like a big deal. Your body is tired, your nerves are frayed, and a lack of sleep makes you less efficient than what you normally would be. Therefore, it doesn't take much to trigger your temper when you're sleep-deprived.

There could be so many possible scenarios and situations that could cause a person to get angry or upset about it. One of the things that you would need to do towards learning how to manage your anger would be to identify the triggers that set you off to learn to recognize them. We can break our anger-response to hormonal levels. The amygdala triggers a response to irritating information or frightening situations. Our "fight or flight" response to annoyances is related to the hormones the brain releases, primarily epinephrine (adrenaline) and norepinephrine (noradrenaline). These hormones result in emotional and physical responses to make us alert and energized. We sometimes call the resulting sensation an "adrenaline rush."

Typically, four responses occur when anger is triggered:

Assertiveness - You're appropriately managing and working through your anger. You're in control and retain your ability to communicate the way you feel towards the person who might have triggered these emotions inside you.

Aggression - This happens when your anger is being unleashed.

Passive-Aggressiveness - On the outside, you're agreeable. On the inside, you're seething and angry but doing your best not to let it show.

Passive - On the surface, you appear calm, and that's because you're storing all your anger and stockpiling it.

Left unchecked, anger could, directly and indirectly, affect your health. It is causing your health problems without you even realizing it. Some examples of how anger is indirectly affecting your health, including increasing your risks of a heart attack because of the constant stress that you feel. It also increases your blood pressure and cholesterol levels, making you prone to having health-related problems because of that stress. It could cause obesity. The way it directly affects your health is by hampering your decision-making process. You can't make rational, appropriate decisions when you're blinded by anger all the time. It drives you to physical injuries too. For example, you could punch something in anger, which ends up hurting you. Or worse, you could punch someone else, which causes physical injury to another person. Neither of which is good, of course.

Anger could drive some towards alcoholic tendencies, lead to road rage, make it difficult to concentrate, and more.

Besides, constant, chronic anger will only increase your chances of contracting heart-related diseases like high blood pressure or heart attacks. Anger is connected to the heart because norepinephrine and epinephrine contract your blood vessels, making your heart pump more difficult. These two hormones also happen to be responsible for increasing glucose and fatty acids in the blood, which only leads to damaged arteries and speeds up atherosclerosis. Luckily, there are healthy ways of learning how to control that anger.

## Chapter 9:   Anger Management

Just like all other basic emotions, anger is designed to convey a specific message to us. That message could be our disapproval of something that has happened or something that someone has done. However, if our first response when angry is to vent or become raging mad, the message gets lost in translation. For this reason, a calm mind and level-head are essential when dealing with anger. Being in a tranquil state of mind allows you to take a step back and objectively evaluate your anger from reason. It also allows you to acknowledge your feelings and validate them

without letting them control you.

Keeping calm when angry, however, is easier said than done. It takes a lot of practice, patience, and maturity to keep yourself from acting out of character when something that triggers rage in us happens. If someone offends you, it is much easier to revenge. In a way, we derive some pleasure from causing suffering to perceived opponents when we feel like they have wronged us. However, in reality, these solutions are illusory, since they do not deal with the real issues and cause of our anger. They can be more detrimental to us and our relationships in the long run. In light of this, we must find healthier ways to control our anger, even when we feel justified in it.

So, what is anger management, and what does it entail? Essentially, anger management is the process of identifying signs that you are becoming angry or frustrated and taking the necessary steps to calm yourself down to deal with your anger more productively. Many people have the misconception that anger management is meant to keep you from feeling angry. Others even think that it is designed to help them suppress feelings. Both of these are poor understandings of the role of anger management. Like we found out earlier, anger is a universal human emotion that all living humans experience at some point in their lives. Also, we already saw why suppressing anger is counterproductive as a long term strategy to manage anger.

The role of anger management is to help you become better at identifying signs that you are becoming frustrated and equip you with the necessary skills to keep your anger under control. A lot of literature has been written about anger and how to deal with it more effectively. Therefore, one can learn the right skills for dealing with frustration from reading books such as this one. However, the most common way people learn anger management is by attending an anger management class or therapy with a counselor.

You will get to learn how to identify the warning signs when you get frustrated, and how you can effectively calm yourself down to approach your anger from the point of strength.

You may be questioning yourself right now, " How do I know if I need anger management classes?" Here are the signs that you need to attend anger management classes to keep them in control.

- You Constantly Feel Like You Need to Suppress Your Anger

While expressing your anger through fits of rage is not the appropriate response for anger, hiding your anger is not a healthy way of coping. If you constantly feel like you need to bottle up your anger, this may point to a lack of proper coping strategy. It may also be that you are afraid of being vulnerable with other people and showing them your true feelings.

Vulnerability is very important in any relationship, as it helps to build trust among individuals. Refusal to be open about one's feelings usually leads to isolation, fear, and distrust. These are not only weak foundations on which to build a relationship, but they can also trigger more feelings of anger and frustration. Therefore, it is essential to take it upon yourself to learn the right coping strategies instead of hiding your feelings of rage.

- You Always Focus on Negative Experiences

Granted, life is very challenging, and everyone will experience negativity in their lives at some point. However, it is important not to allow the bad things in our lives to rid us of our joy and vitality. If you constantly focus only on your life's negative experiences, you get distracted from actually living your life to the fullest potential. You may also find it a lot tougher to appreciate everyday living's simple pleasures, such as having a comfortable roof over your head and people who love you. You, therefore, need to learn the right coping strategies when angry to prevent your anger from becoming habitual.

- You Constantly Struggle with Feelings of Hostility and Irritation

If you constantly struggle with uncomfortable feelings of irritation and hostility towards others, you need to learn anger management skills. While life is not perfect every day, many things make it worth the experience. If you are perennially irritated by the state of affairs in your life, this may point too deep-seated anger issues that need to be resolved as soon as possible.

- You Constantly Find Yourself in Arguments which Further Trigger Your Anger

There are many instances in life when you will find yourself justifiably angry at someone for something they did. However, if you always find yourself in heated confrontations with people, this could sign an underlying anger problem. It could also simply be a sign that the strategies you use to deal with your anger are ineffective. Perhaps your first response when angry is to blame the other person or throw a temper tantrum. Maybe you even find yourself engaging in abusive exchanges with the objects of your frustration. These strategies of coping with anger are very inappropriate since they only trigger more angry reactions from you. Instead, it is important to find a way of calming yourself down enough to deal with the issue with an objective mind.

- You Engage in Physical Violence when Angry

While anger is a very normal reaction that may provoke feelings of aggression, using violence to deal with anger is inappropriate. Physically abusive responses when angry can be very damaging to your health, reputation as well as relationships. It can also lead to very serious legal consequences, such as getting sued or imprisoned for abuse. If you find yourself prone to committing acts of violence when angry, you should immediately seek professional help. Through counseling and attending anger management classes, you can break this cycle of poor anger management and learn to express your frustration in healthier ways that do not involve violence.

- You Manifest Out-of-Control Behavior when Angry

Perhaps you are not outrightly violent towards other people when angry. However, you may tend to smash or break things when angry. This is still not an appropriate response or strategy to deal with anger and frustration. This type of behavior fails to address the real cause of the anger, and only reinforces the idea that showing aggression will make the anger go away. The truth is that it doesn't work. The only effective way of dealing with anger is getting to the root cause and harnessing the emotion in positive ways.

- You Avoid Certain Situations Because of Fear of Getting Angry

Another tell-tale sign that you need lessons in anger management is you find yourself constantly avoiding scenarios that may trigger your anger. Perhaps you don't like going to parties with your spouse because they always leave you alone to chat with the other people. Maybe you avoid talking to one of your close friends because you feel they are too judgmental.

Whichever the case, the temptation to avoid any scenario that may trigger your anger can be too strong to resist. However, opting out of certain situations due to fear of getting frustrated is not an effective way of dealing with your anger. For one, it shifts the responsibility to the other person, thereby diminishing your power to take responsibility for your emotions. It also only covers up pent up frustration, which continues to simmer without your awareness. This can eventually erupt in very damaging ways, both to you and your relationships.

Anger management classes are typically designed to help people develop the skills to notice when they get angry and take the necessary steps to deal with the emotion appropriately. Usually, the classes are conducted as one-on-one sessions or group sessions with a counselor or therapist. Depending on your needs, the anger management program may take a few days, weeks, or even months. Therefore, you need to be patient and consider the whole experience as a learning process.

When you first begin attending anger management classes, the first thing you will learn is how to identify stressors and triggers of anger. By identifying the early warning signs of anger, you can begin to understand its causes and figure out how to control it. Stressors are typically those things that cause frustration in your life and trigger pent up anger. These may include frustration with a child who behaves poorly, financial problems, or coworkers who constantly gossip about you.

Apart from identifying the triggers, anger management classes will help teach you how to pick up on anger symptoms. As we found out earlier, physiological symptoms of anger vary between individuals. You may, therefore, not manifest the same symptoms as someone else when angry. While one person may experience an increased heart rate and sweat when angry, another person may feel a tight-knot in their stomach when upset. Anger management classes will help you identify the physical symptoms of anger as they present uniquely in your body.

Beginner's anger management is also meant to help you recognize the signs that your anger is on the rise. Perhaps you may feel like you want to yell at your anger's perceived object, or you feel the need to keep quiet to avoid a heated confrontation. Being aware of the physical reactions happening in your body will allow you to take a step back and carefully evaluate your anger before proceeding with an appropriate response.

## Chapter 10: How To Heal Your Body And Soul: Emotional Freedom Techniques

What is emotional freedom? And why do we need it? Who is it helpful for, what does it help with? Is there a place in the fast-paced serious world? And how is it achieved?

Emotional freedom is that much-desired and increasingly difficult state of harmony and peace. A state in which we are free from the influence of our negative emotions on our psyche, our decisions, our deeds, our communication. We do not stop to feel emotions, but we can distinguish ourselves from them and their influence on our decisions, reactions and actions. We are already independent of the filter of emotions that distorts our perceptions and experiences!

Why do we need emotional freedom? When we are free from the effects of increasingly stressful external factors, we are independent. Throughout our life, the accumulated experiences, starting from childhood—traumatic experiences, disappointments, insults—create several sabotaging and limiting beliefs in the subconscious. The unpleasant feeling always experienced is strongly associated with the nervous system, with the body's entire internal biochemistry and becomes an integral part of us. It arises with a new limiting force in every situation, resembling that past unpleasant moment. When we are under the influence of a negative emotion, we are dependent on it because of an experience in the present or the past. They establish our mood, self-esteem, decisions, and actions or inactions. Emotion creates a filter on our perceptions that distorts reality. We interpret and feel what is happening from the standpoint of painful memories and beliefs of the past.

So we are dependent on our fears, on the feeling that we are not good enough, that people do not accept us and reject us, humiliate us, and threaten us. Or are we just unsure that we won't do it, that we don't deserve it. Or they get us into a real hell of panic, anxiety, and obsessive thoughts. Self-sabotaging subconscious beliefs can truly upset our lives. Often, unresolved emotional conflicts, when seeking a solution, manifest themselves as illnesses in our physical body.

Release from negative experiences, perceptions, emotions, fears, and sabotaging beliefs allows us to have a better quality of life. We feel better physically, communicate with ease, and meet our daily challenges. We can improve every area of our lives. Emotional freedom enables us to recognize challenges, work consciously. and direct our emotions.

EFT encompasses everything that happens simultaneously in the mind, emotions, and body to release and transform it. EFT and other energy psychology techniques are often used to achieve excellence in business, sports, or in personal. They reveal and eliminate subconscious internal conflicts and limiting beliefs that hinder our success and realization.

The EFT has one great advantage—because of its simplicity, it is quickly mastered by anyone and easily applied in all situations and at any time—true freedom at the tip of your fingers! As its creator says: "Try it on whatever comes to your mind! Especially when nothing else helps!"

Everywhere in the civilized world—for over thirty years—leading specialists, therapists, and medical professionals have been using EFTs in individual and group practices. EFTs are becoming more accessible, understandable, and easily applicable not only by the world's greats in sports, politics, and business. EFTs are gentle, easy to understand, and easy to implement by anyone!

What is the evidence that it works? EFT and Matrix Rearrangement have been the subject of serious research. The method is based on fully scientifically recognized and proven approaches—from acupuncture to cognitive therapies and perceptions from different psychotherapy units and new medicine. Measurements and studies with apparatus recording changes in brain activity and stress levels have recorded a remarkable turn in the course of one or more sessions.

The results from practitioners around the world are amazing. It deals with people experiencing disasters and huge losses, with war veterans, with children with attention deficit disorder and hyperactivity disorder. Therapeutic sessions improve and heal the following: anxiety, allergies, panic attacks and anxiety, addictions, inability to cope with life's challenges, weight loss, lack of faith and purpose, complete change and release of negative memories, depression, terminal illnesses, successful conception and childbirth after unsuccessful in vitro procedures, clearing of severe birth memories and relationships, intolerance to life, consequences of sexual abuse, withdrawal from bad habits, and traumas—the events that have left a swelling in life . . . the memory has changed.

Who needs emotional freedom? Emotional freedom techniques are one of the most popular and accessible methods of energy psychology. Created by engineer Gary Craig in 1995, energy psychology is a line of collective psychotherapy methods, coaching, and other healing approaches based on the tradition of healing the body-mind system, dating back five thousand years ago. The EP blends the bio-energy foundations of these traditions with best-in-class psychological practice, and has in the past thirty-five years been further validated by clinical experience with millions of clients around the world and supported by research at numerous universities.

The energy psychology methods gently and quickly release the body-mind system from negative perceptions and stressful events frozen over time in it. These events are the reason for the negative way in which one sees the world and the people around him, or the basis of outdated programs on how to experience and regulate his emotions and how to enter into relationships with other people.

Also known as Tapping Techniques, Meridian Tapping, EFT Tapping, and more, they combine the achievements of cognitive (analytical) therapies in Western medical science with ancient Eastern knowledge of the body and the subtle energies that flow into it. While modern Western medicine underestimates the impact of thoughts and feelings on the onset of illnesses, and verbal psychotherapies ignore the body's physiological reactions when experiencing negative emotions, TEC focuses on what is happening simultaneously in the mind and body to release it.

**Techniques For Emotional Freedom**

Emotional freedom techniques points based on ancient acupuncture, the technique is a tapping of ten acupuncture points on the face and body while experiencing negative emotion, which helps to quickly, within minutes, release the unpleasant feeling. Medical research has found that this tapping sends a soothing signal to the brain's center responsible for our fight or flight response. This signal breaks the link between the thought, feeling, and physical sensation of the body that corresponds to that negative feeling or physical pain. The erasure of negative feeling restores the capacity for rational thinking and the ability to find solutions. Based on the EFT, much deeper and with astonishing results, is the Matrix Rearrange technique.

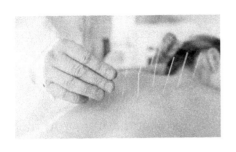

# Chapter 11:    Stress And Worry

Stress alone is responsible for tens of thousands of deaths every year. Stress does more harm than many diseases and leaves countless families grieving the loss of a loved one. This is why you must take active steps towards reducing your stress levels.

## Taking Responsibility For Your Stress

 Stress is something you have some control over and, therefore, must take responsibility for. The more you take responsibility for it, the better you'll be able to reduce it.

Stress happens for various reasons and manifests in numerous situations. The traffic jam on your way to work, a business presentation, tensions with your boss, or frequent disputes with your spouse all constitute potential stress sources. There are two ways you can reduce stress:

- By avoiding situations you perceive as stressful, and
- By becoming better at dealing with stressful situations.

We'll see how you can use these methods to reduce your stress levels.

## How You Can Use Stress To Grow

Exercise - Make a list of your major sources of stress

Let's look at specific situations that are sources of stress for you. Using the workbook, write down what causes the most stress in your typical week. Come up with at least ten things.

## Reframing Stress

Emotions arise as a result of your interpretation of events. The mere fact you experience stress (or any other emotion) means you've added your interpretation to what is happening. Otherwise, you would have a stress-free life.

Now, look at your list of stressful situations. For each situation ask yourself the following questions:

- Is that situation stressful in itself?
- What do I need to believe to experience stress in that specific situation?
- What would I need to believe to reduce or remove stress in that particular situation?

Let's say you're stuck in a traffic jam and you find it stressful.

Is that situation stressful in itself?

No, not necessarily. The traffic jam exists and there is nothing wrong with it, per se.

What would I need to believe to experience stress in that specific situation?

I would need to believe:

- There shouldn't be any traffic jams, and therefore, something is wrong.
- The traffic jam is a stressful event in itself.
- I should be where I need to go, instead of being stuck in traffic.

75

- I can do something about it.

What would I need to believe to reduce/remove stress in that particular situation?

I would need to believe that:

- A traffic jam is a normal event like anything else.
- I don't necessarily have to experience stress just because I'm stuck in traffic.
- I'm here caught in a traffic jam and I don't need to be there (wherever I want to go), for a while.
- I can't do anything about it, so I might as well enjoy it, or at least don't stress over it.

**Dealing With Worry**

Worry differs from stress as it isn't the result of something you experience in the present, but a concern you have regarding events from the past or events that may happen in the future. You experience stress when you face a stressful situation in the present moment.

For instance, a stressful situation would be being stuck in a traffic jam or having your boss yell at you. Worrying would be remembering (past) or anticipating/imagining these stressful situations (future). Interestingly, most of your worries are unnecessary for the following reasons:

- They happened in the past and there's absolutely nothing you can do about them, and
- They may happen in the future and you can't control the future.

Exercise - Make a list of your worries

Make a list of things you worry about (past or future). They may be similar to the things you wrote in the previous exercise. Examples of things you may worry about are:

- Your health
- Your financial situations
- Your work
- Your relationships, and
- Your family.

Now, write at least ten things you tend to worry about in a typical week.

## Sorting Out Your Worries

Constant worry results from trying to control events over which you have no control. When you do so, you create unnecessary stress in your life. To deal with stress and overcome chronic worries more effectively, you must learn to sort out worries. An effective way to do this is to separate the things you have control over from the things you have no control over. You can divide your worries into three separate categories:

- Things you have control over
- Things you have some control over, and
- Things you have no control over whatsoever.

1. Things you have control over:

This category includes things such as your actions and behaviors. For instance, you can choose what to say and how to say it. You can also decide what actions you'll take to achieve your goals.

2. Things you have some control over:

There are things you have only limited control over such as a competition or a job interview. You can't be certain you'll win a tennis match but you do have some control over its outcome. For instance, you can choose to train harder or hire a great coach. Similarly, you can prepare for a job interview by conducting extensive research about the company you apply to or doing a mock interview. You don't, however, have absolute control over the outcome of the interview.

3. Things you have no control over:

Unfortunately, there are also many things you have no control over. These are things such as the weather, the economy, or traffic jams.

Exercise - Sort out your worries

Look at your list of stressful situations. Next to each item, put C (control), SC (Some control), or NC (No control). This simple act of sorting out your worries already helps reduce them. As you identify things you have no control over, you can let go of your urge to worry.

Now, for things you have (some) control over, write down what you could do about it. What concrete actions could you take to alleviate them?

For things you have no control over, can you let go of your need to control them instead of accepting them?

## Taking One Hundred Percent Responsibility For Your Stress And Worries

What if you had more control over your worries than you believe? Look at the situations you have no control over and ask yourself, "If I had control over them, what would I do? What would it look like? And how could I prevent them from happening?"

Often, you'll realize you have some control over these situations. This can be by changing, reframing or eliminating them from your life.

Let's say you identified traffic jams as something you have no control over. This sounds reasonable. Once you're caught in the traffic jam, you can't do much about it. But, could you do things differently? For instance, could you leave home earlier or take a different route?

What about reframing the situation? Instead of escaping the situation mentally, you could choose to be fully present by making traffic jams a productive part of your day. You could then make the most of it by listening to audiobooks. Imagine how much you could learn if you listened to audiobooks every working day for an entire year.

Go over your list and look for things you have no control over. Write down what you could do to change, reframe or eliminate these events.